Oxford Primary Skills

Reading and writing

Tamzin Thompson

4

T0352848

Unit	Structures	Vocabulary	Skills
1 Eating round the world page 4	We use chopsticks and we sometimes use spoons. Look! I'm using chopsticks.	fry steam chopsticks serving dish reach napkin	📖: Magazine feature ✏️: Punctuation review A special meal in my country
2 Making music page 8	Mozart travelled around Europe. As a young boy, Pavarotti listened to singers on the radio.	piano flute orchestra composer conductor opera	📖: Biographical article ✏️: Linking expressions Short biography
3 My favourite sport page 12	Football is more exciting than basketball. I like volleyball because it's exciting.	pitch goalpost goalkeeper kit fans hoop	📖: Playscript ✏️: Adjectives and adverbs My favourite sport
4 Future inventions page 16	There will be escalators and glass lifts. Will the museum be small? No, it won't.	escalator lift walkway audio guide laboratory display	📖: Plans for a new museum ✏️: *be like / look like* My future invention
5 Happy holidays page 20	How many decks are there on the ship? There's a swimming pool and there's a climbing wall.	deck shopping mall ice rink whirlpool climbing wall gym	📖: Holiday brochure ✏️: Structures for describing My dream hotel
6 Watching wildlife page 24	The mothers go to the sea to find food for their chicks. Chameleons are unusual animals because …	cameraman lay eggs balance hatch chick feed	📖: Magazine article ✏️: *un-* prefix An animal and its characteristics
7 Survival tips page 28	Have you ever been in the jungle? It's very important to travel with a friend.	hill insect repellent branch boil insects happy thoughts	📖: Survival handbook ✏️: Structures for advising Travel advice
8 Growing things page 32	You should plant vegetables in a sunny place. You shouldn't plant the seeds close together.	soil seed bulbs rake dig pots	📖: Gardening advice ✏️: *because* and *so* Advice on growing sunflowers
9 Heroes page 36	Jake, who lives next door to us, is … We've known him since we moved to this street.	dive drag trapped escape rescue put out	📖: News stories ✏️: Relative clauses My hero
10 Story time page 40	Anna and Jack were staying at their Grandpa's house. When Grandpa went shopping, Jack had an idea.	shed broken mend drawer polish shiny	📖: Fiction ✏️: Punctuation of dialogue A story with dialogue
More words page 44		Five extra words for each unit	

OXFORD
UNIVERSITY PRESS

Teaching notes

The *Oxford Primary Skills* series is designed to be used alongside a coursebook to develop reading and writing skills, and uses a balance of familiar and new language in different contexts.

Each level of *Reading and writing* is made up of ten units that are designed to be used in order. The texts progress in length and the skills practised progress in difficulty through the book. The units follow a grammar and vocabulary syllabus designed to be consistent with what the children are learning in their language lessons.

Reading

There are a variety of reading text types through the course to expose children to different types of English in use. Children will be motivated by their ability to read and understand 'real' text types such as websites and magazine articles that have been graded to their level. Children develop the skills of reading and listening for gist and detail, both of which are essential for complete communicative competence.

Some of the text types they will encounter are, amongst others:
stories, magazine and newspaper articles, posters, leaflets, websites, factfiles, reports.

Writing

In the Writing section of each unit, the children practise punctuation, syntax and text structuring, and are given the opportunity to write different types of text, often about themselves, closely following a model text that will support them in structuring their writing. Their writing confidence will develop as they find they have written, amongst others: emails, descriptions, interviews, biographies, diary entries, website profiles, stories.

More words

At the back of the book is an optional section of vocabulary extension exercises that can be used to augment the number of words the children learn in each unit from six to eleven. The extra words are consistent with the topic of the unit and can be used, by those children who complete the activities, in the Writing task at the end of each unit.

It is to be stressed that these words are optional and it is perfectly possible to complete the course without using this additional section.

Tour of a unit

Each unit is topic-based and the topics are consistent with areas the children will be covering in their English language coursebooks and in other subject areas. The units are structured to offer the children support in developing their reading and writing skills. Every unit follows the same structure:

Reading and Comprehension
pages 1 and 2 of each unit
The six new words are introduced in picture form at the top of the first page. Use the pictures to teach the words which will form the basis for the Vocabulary work in the unit and will also appear in the Reading text.

The Reading text follows the new words. There is also a recorded version of this text on the Teacher's CD.

When you start to teach a new text, approach it in three stages: *pre-reading*, *reading for gist*, and *reading for detail*. Explain that children do not have to understand every word

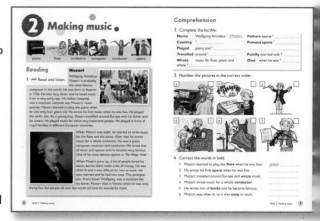

to do this. By focusing on the language they do understand, it is possible to guess or use logic to work out the meaning of the rest.

Pre-reading. This stage is about looking for clues to help the children piece together the meaning of the text. This includes looking at the pictures and text style to guess what type of text it is and what it is likely to be about. Ask the children to give suggestions about what they think the text will say before they start to read.

Reading for gist. Play the recording twice while the children follow the text in their books. They do not need to be able to read every word independently, but be able to read carefully enough to understand the gist. Ask some simple comprehension questions to ensure they have understood the general points.

Reading for detail. This stage will take place as you go onto the Comprehension page. Go through the first comprehension activity with the class so that the children know what information to look for in the text. Give them time to read the text again to find the answers. Have a class feedback session. Then let the children answer the questions on their own or do the following exercise/s together as a class if you prefer.

Vocabulary

page 3 of each unit

The vocabulary exercises give the children the opportunity to practise the new words learnt earlier in the unit. The vocabulary items are practised in the context of simple, graded language structures and alongside other vocabulary items that they are likely to recognize from their coursebook or from the context of the reading text.

On the Vocabulary pages in this level, the children are introduced to the concept of word definition. This lays the basis for later development of the skills of dictionary use as they progress as language learners.

At the bottom of the third page of the unit, you will see directions to the *More words* section for that unit. For those wishing to further extend the children's vocabulary, this is the stage in the unit where these new words should be taught and practised. This allows the children the option to use them in their writing task on the final page of the unit.

Writing

page 4 of each unit

The Writing page begins with a model text that the children should read. Apply the same approach as for the Reading text.

Look for clues in the picture and the style of the text for what type of text it might be and what they think they might be asked to write.

Read the text together as a class to see if they were right with their predictions.

Then move on to the exercise following the text. This focuses on a writing skill that will help them to complete the final writing task of the unit. Some examples of these are, amongst others:
punctuation, linking expressions, giving advice, relative clauses, recognizing adjectives and adverbs.

Do feedback as a class before they move on to the writing task.

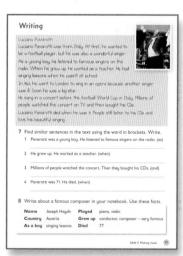

The writing tasks are very well-supported with useful words and phrases given in the yellow boxes so the children are not pushed beyond their level of competence. They are based very closely on the model text above, and the children should be encouraged to refer back to the text you have read together to complete the final exercise of the unit in their notebooks.

For more extensive teaching notes and answer key, refer to www.oup.com/elt/teachersclub/young-learners

1 Eating round the world

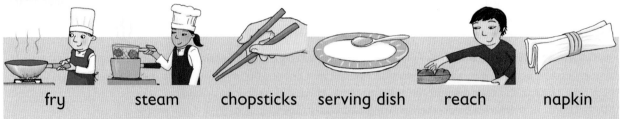

fry   steam   chopsticks   serving dish   reach   napkin

Reading

1 🔊01 Read and listen.

Eating in China

Hi. I'm Lin, I'm eleven and I'm from China. Chinese food is really delicious. We eat a lot of rice, noodles, vegetables and meat. We fry or steam a lot of our food. It is very healthy.

In China, people don't usually eat with knives and forks. Instead we use chopsticks and we sometimes use spoons.

We usually eat from big serving dishes. We put them in the middle of the table, but we sometimes serve portions of rice in small bowls. In China, we don't think it's rude to reach across the table to take food from serving dishes.

We do think it is rude to take the last piece of food from a serving dish for yourself. We offer it to another person instead. That is very polite.

When your bowl is empty, someone gives you more food. When you are full, you put your hand over your bowl or leave some food in your bowl. We don't put our chopsticks on top of our bowls. We put them on the table next to us when we finish eating. We don't use napkins, but we usually clean our hands with hot towels at the end of the meal.

Do you like Chinese food? Is it very different from food in your country?

Comprehension

2 Read and tick (✔) or cross (✗).

1 Her name is Lin and she's from China.   ✔

2 Lin thinks Chinese food is delicious.   ☐

3 People in China always use knives and forks to eat.   ☐

4 Chinese people fry or steam a lot of their food.   ☐

5 It's rude to take the last piece of food from a serving dish.   ☐

6 People usually use napkins in China.   ☐

3 Match. Write the number.

1 It isn't rude to reach across the table in China.

2 In China, people eat with chopsticks.

3 People sometimes serve rice in small bowls in China.

4 Chinese people use hot towels at the end of a meal.

5 In China, people put serving dishes in the middle of the table.

6 Chinese people eat rice, vegetables and meat.

4 Read and write *Yes, they do.* or *No, they don't.*

1 Do people in China usually use knives and forks?   <u>No, they don't.</u>

2 Do people in China eat a lot of rice and vegetables?   _____

3 Do people in China eat from serving dishes?   _____

4 Do people in China use napkins at the end of a meal?   _____

Vocabulary

5 Complete the sentences with the words in the box.

> waiter   menu   ~~chopsticks~~   fry   napkin   reach
> serving dish   steam   empty   polite

1 Chinese people usually eat with <u>chopsticks.</u>

2 We usually eat from a _____ in the middle of the table.

3 I like to _____ vegetables because it's healthy.

4 In China, it isn't rude to _____ across the table.

5 British people use a _____ at the end of a meal.

6 Chinese people _____ a lot of their food.

7 The _____ is the person who brings food in a restaurant.

8 In a restaurant, you look at a _____ to choose your food.

9 In China, when your plate is _____, someone will serve you more food

10 It is _____ to offer someone else the last piece of food on a
serving dish.

6 Circle.

This is my favourite restaurant. The food here is great. I eat here with my family.

Look! I'm using ¹(chopsticks)/ spoons.

My sister is eating a ² glass / bowl of salad, and my mum is drinking a ³ cup / plate of coffee. There is a big ⁴ knife / serving dish on our table.

There are two customers at the next table. The woman is looking at the ⁵ chopsticks / menu. There is a ⁶ towel / napkin on her table and there is some bread on the table, too. The man is ⁷ steaming / reaching to take some bread.

More words on page 44

Writing

Do you eat special food at New Year? I live in Japan. We make special dishes for New Year. We use fish, rice and lots of vegetables. The different dishes mean health and happiness for the New Year. – **Yuko, Tokyo**

I'm from Spain. At New Year, we always eat twelve grapes. The grapes are for the twelve months of the year. We eat the grapes because they are sweet, and we want every month in the new year to be sweet, too! – **Maria, Madrid**

In Greece we make a special cake for New Year. We put a coin in the cake. When we cut the cake we all look for the coin. The coin means a happy new year for you and your family. – **Yianni, Athens**

Use **.** at the end of a sentence: My name is Kate**.**

Use **,** in lists of three or more things: We eat vegetables**,** rice and meat.

Use **'** in short forms: I**'**m from the UK.

Use **?** at the end of questions: Do you eat special food in your country**?**

Use **capital letters** at the beginning of a sentence and for names, cities, countries and special days: **T**om loves **N**ew **Y**ear in **F**rance.

7 Rewrite the sentences with punctuation.

1 its new years day tomorrow <u>It's New Year's Day tomorrow.</u>

2 im from australia _____

3 we usually eat fish vegetables and fruit _____

4 does maria live in italy _____

5 mike sam and lisa are from the usa _____

6 what do you eat on new year's eve _____

8 Write about what you eat at New Year in your notebook. Use these words and phrases.

• *I'm from …* • *At New Year, we …* • *We sometimes …* • *We … because …*

2 Making music

piano

flute

orchestra

composer

conductor

opera

Reading

1 🔊02 Read and listen.

Mozart

Wolfgang Amadeus Mozart is probably the most famous composer in the world. He was born in Austria in 1756. He was very clever and he loved music from a very early age. His father, Leopold, was a musician. Leopold was Mozart's music teacher. Mozart learned to play the piano when he was only four years old. He wrote his first music when he was five. He played the violin, too. As a young boy, Mozart travelled around Europe with his father and his sisters. He played music for some very important people. He played in front of royal families in different European countries.

When Mozart was eight, he started to write music for the flute and the piano. After that he wrote music for a whole orchestra. He was a great composer, musician and conductor. He wrote lots of music and operas and he became very famous. One of his most famous operas is 'The Magic Flute'.

When Mozart grew up, a lot of people loved his music, but he didn't make a lot of money. He was often ill and it was difficult for him to work. He was married and he had two sons. The youngest son, Franz Xaver Wolfgang, was a musician like his father. Mozart died in Vienna when he was only thirty-five, but people all over the world still love his wonderful music.

Comprehension

2 Complete the factfile.

Name	Wolfgang Amadeus [1] _Mozart_	**Father's name** [6] _____
Country	[2] _____	**Famous opera** [7] _____
Played	piano and [3] _____	_____
Travelled	around [4] _____	**Family** married with [8] _____
Wrote	music for flute, piano and whole [5] _____	**Died** when he was [9] _____

3 Number the pictures in the correct order.

a

b

c

d [1]

e

f

4 Correct the words in bold.

1 Mozart learned to play the **flute** when he was four.   _piano_

2 He wrote his first **opera** when he was five.   _____

3 Mozart travelled around Europe and **wrote** music.   _____

4 Mozart wrote music for a whole **conductor**.   _____

5 He wrote lots of **books** and he became famous.   _____

6 Mozart was often ill, so it was **easy** to work.   _____

Vocabulary

5 Match the definitions with the words in the box.

> violin   audience   orchestra   conductor   ~~flute~~   opera   drums   composer

1 You blow it with your mouth.   <u>flute</u>
2 Lots of different instruments playing together.   _____
3 A man or woman who writes music.   _____
4 You hit these with sticks or with your hands.   _____
5 A man or woman who stands in front of the orchestra.   _____
6 A type of play where people sing the words.   _____
7 The people who sit and watch a play or concert.   _____
8 A string instrument you play with a bow.   _____

6 Complete the sentences with the words in the box.

> drums   flute   guitar   ~~orchestra~~   piano   trumpet   violin

1 The <u>orchestra</u> is on the stage.
2 The boy in the blue jumper is playing the _____.
3 This girl in the white dress is playing the _____.
4 The girl in the red dress is playing the _____.
5 The boy in the green jumper is playing the _____.
6 Two girls are playing the _____.
7 The boy in the yellow jumper is playing the _____.

More words on page 44

Writing

Luciano Pavarotti

Luciano Pavarotti was from Italy. At first, he wanted to be a football player, but he was also a wonderful singer.

As a young boy, he listened to famous singers on the radio. When he grew up, he worked as a teacher. He had singing lessons when he wasn't at school.

In 1963, he went to London to sing in an opera because another singer was ill. Soon he was a big star.

He sang in a concert before the football World Cup in Italy. Millions of people watched the concert on TV and then bought his CDs.

Luciano Pavarotti died when he was 71. People still listen to his CDs and love his beautiful singing.

7 Find similar sentences in the text using the word in brackets. Write.

1 Pavarotti was a young boy. He listened to famous singers on the radio. (as)

_____

2 He grew up. He worked as a teacher. (when)

_____

3 Millions of people watched the concert. Then they bought his CDs. (and)

_____

4 Pavarotti was 71. He died. (when)

_____

8 Write about a famous composer in your notebook. Use these facts.

Name	Joseph Haydn	**Played**	piano, violin
Country	Austria	**Grew up**	conductor, composer – very famous
As a boy	singing lessons	**Died**	77

3 My favourite sport

 pitch  goalposts  goalkeeper  kit  fans hoop

Reading

1 🔊03 Read and listen.

Tom and Emma are in the park.

Tom: This is my new football kit. Let's play football in the park, Emma.

Emma: No thanks. I don't like football.

Tom: Why not, Emma? I know you're a basketball fan. But you can like both of them. I think football is more exciting than basketball.

Emma: But I can't play football. It's too difficult for me.

Tom: No, it isn't. It's easy! There are goalposts at the end of the pitch. You just kick the ball and you try to score a goal.

Emma: It's not easy for me! Basketball is much easier than football. You throw the ball through the hoop. That's all. I'm good at throwing. I'm not very good at kicking.

Tom: OK. You can be the goalkeeper. The goalkeeper throws the ball.

Emma: OK then. Let's play football.

Tom and Emma go onto the pitch with their friends.

Tom: Throw the ball, Emma!

Emma: OK. Ready? Here it is!

Tom: Wow, Emma! You are really good at throwing! Maybe that was a bit too far …

Emma: Oh no! Sorry.

Comprehension

2 Write *Tom* or *Emma*.

1 <u>Tom</u> wants to play football in the park.

2 _____ thinks football is more exciting than basketball.

3 _____ is a basketball fan and doesn't like football.

4 _____ can be the goalkeeper because she is good at throwing.

5 _____ has got a new football kit.

6 _____ thinks basketball is easier than football.

3 Copy the sentences into the table.

> ~~The goalkeeper can throw the ball.~~   All the players can throw the ball.
> There are two hoops.   There are goalposts.
> You can kick the ball.   You must be good at throwing.

🏀 **In basketball …**	⚽ **In football …**
	The goalkeeper can throw the ball.

4 Answer the questions with *Yes, he / she does.* or *No, he / she doesn't.*

1 Does Emma want to play football? <u>No, she doesn't.</u>

2 Does Tom think football is exciting? _____

3 Does Emma like basketball? _____

4 Does Tom throw the ball? _____

5 Does Emma throw the ball? _____

Vocabulary

5 Complete the sentences with the words in the box.

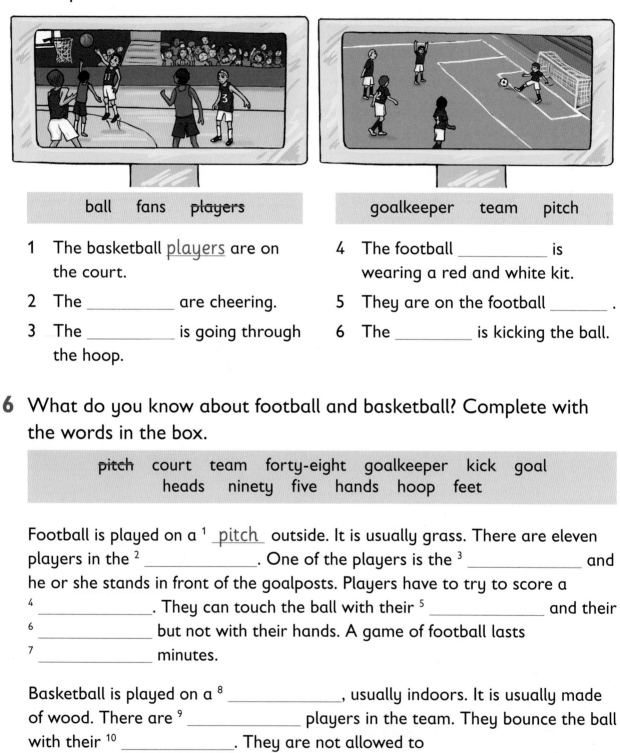

ball	fans	~~players~~

1 The basketball <u>players</u> are on the court.

2 The _____ are cheering.

3 The _____ is going through the hoop.

goalkeeper	team	pitch

4 The football _____ is wearing a red and white kit.

5 They are on the football _____.

6 The _____ is kicking the ball.

6 What do you know about football and basketball? Complete with the words in the box.

~~pitch~~ court team forty-eight goalkeeper kick goal
heads ninety five hands hoop feet

Football is played on a ¹ <u>pitch</u> outside. It is usually grass. There are eleven players in the ² _____. One of the players is the ³ _____ and he or she stands in front of the goalposts. Players have to try to score a ⁴ _____. They can touch the ball with their ⁵ _____ and their ⁶ _____ but not with their hands. A game of football lasts ⁷ _____ minutes.

Basketball is played on a ⁸ _____, usually indoors. It is usually made of wood. There are ⁹ _____ players in the team. They bounce the ball with their ¹⁰ _____. They are not allowed to ¹¹ _____ the ball. Players have to try to get the ball through a ¹² _____. A game of basketball lasts ¹³ _____ minutes.

More words on page 45

Writing

My favourite sport

My favourite sport is volleyball. It's great.
You play volleyball on a court. You need a ball and a net.
There are two teams and there are six players on each team.
They take turns to serve. The players move very fast. They
usually hit the ball with their hands or arms. They hit it very
hard. They hit the ball over the net. The teams score points
when the ball hits the ground on the other team's side of the
net. I like volleyball because it's exciting. It's good exercise and it's lots of fun.

Use adjectives to describes nouns: I like volleyball because it's **exciting**.

Use adverbs to describe verbs: The players move very **fast**.

7 Circle the adjectives and underline the adverbs.

1 The fans cheered <u>loudly</u> when the team scored a goal.

2 I think football is very (exciting).

3 The children laughed happily when they saw their friends.

4 John can run very fast.

5 Do you like my new football kit?

6 Please play your music quietly.

7 These trainers are very expensive.

8 Why are you walking so slowly?

8 Write about your favourite sport in your notebook.

Use these words and phrases.

• *My favourite sport is ...* • *You need ...* • *There are ...* • *I like ... because ...*

4 Future inventions

 escalator   lift    walkway   audio guide    laboratory   display

Reading

1 04 Read and listen.

The Museum of Future Inventions

What do you think will be invented in the future? Do you have any ideas? Soon, there will be a Museum of Future Inventions near London. At the museum you will be able to see models of the machines, cars and robots of the future.

The museum will be very big. There will be modern escalators and beautiful glass lifts. Visitors will move through the museum on moving walkways. They will listen to audio guides to find out about the things in the museum. Some of the robots will talk to you. They will be able to talk in a lot of different languages.

There will be cinemas, laboratories, classrooms, a café and a gift shop in the museum. At the gift shop there will be fantastic things to buy for your friends and family. There will also be a Young Inventor Laboratory for children, with displays of new inventions. Children will make their own future inventions in the laboratory.

In the Technology room you will see displays of computers, TVs and games consoles of the future. There will be very small computers that you can wear like a watch. There will be games consoles and TVs with 3D images. There will be tiny phones you will wear in your ears.

Do you have an idea for a future invention? Why not send it to us? We will send you a Future Inventor T-shirt. We will send the best ideas to the museum and they will put them on the walls of the Young Inventor Laboratory for everyone to see.

Comprehension

2 Read and tick (✔) or cross (✘).

1   The museum is open now.   **✘**

2   There will be models of machines in the museum. ☐

3   The museum will be small. ☐

4   There will be a shop in the museum. ☐

5   Children will learn about animals in the Young Inventor Laboratory. ☐

6   There will be computers you wear in your ears. ☐

7   You can send your ideas for inventions to the magazine. ☐

3 Write a sentence from the text for each picture.

1   Visitors will move through the museum on moving walkways.

2   _____ _____

3   _____ _____ _____

4   _____ _____ _____

4 Answer the questions.

1   Where will the museum be? Near London.

2   Will there be robots in the museum? _____

3   Will the museum be small? _____

4   How will visitors move through the museum? _____

5   Why will visitors listen to audio guides? _____

6   Where will children make their own inventions? _____

7   How will you wear computers in the future? _____

8   Where will you wear tiny phones in the future? _____

Vocabulary

5 Read the definitions and circle.

1 A (lift) / *display* carries people up and down to other floors in a building.

2 A moving staircase is called an *audio guide* / *escalator*.

3 A *walkway* / *display* is a collection of pictures or objects to look at on a wall or table.

4 Something you listen to that gives you information is an *inventor* / *audio guide*.

5 You walk on a moving *walkway* / *escalator* as a way of moving quickly along the ground.

6 Someone who designs or makes something that didn't exist before is called *a professor* / *an inventor*.

7 A room where scientists work and do experiments is a *laboratory* / *kitchen*.

8 An *invention* / *laboratory* is a new machine that someone has made for the first time.

9 Something electronic you play with on your own or with friends is a *jigsaw* / *games console*.

6 Complete the text with the words in the box.

| audio guide   display   housework   inventor   laboratory   planets |
| robots   ~~spaceship~~ |

Last week, we went to the Science Museum. It was great.

My brother and I sat in a ¹ <u>spaceship</u> and we saw the moon and all the ² _____.

Mum looked at a ³ _____ of clocks and listened to an ⁴ _____.

Dad and I watched an ⁵ _____ making a machine in a ⁶ _____.

Then, we all looked at lots of ⁷ _____. They were cooking and they were doing ⁸ _____.

More words on page 45

Writing

My future invention

I think we will have special shoes like these in the future. They will look like trainers and they will be very comfortable. Everyone will be able to wear them, even children and old people.

The shoes will have wheels, like rollerskates, so they will help us to move around quickly. They will also lift us off the ground when we want to jump over things or fly to a different place.

These shoes are a great idea because we won't need bikes or cars to travel around the town. They will be good for the environment.

7 Write *like*, *looks like* or *look like*.

1 These special shoes <u>look like</u> trainers.

2 They will have wheels, _____ rollerskates.

3 That car is amazing. It _____ a spaceship.

4 The museum will have walkways, _____ an airport.

5 When my mum wears sunglasses, she _____ a film star.

6 Chinese noodles are long and thin, _____ spaghetti.

7 Jack and Jim _____ their dad, but he is taller than them.

8 Write about a future invention in your notebook. Use the notes below or imagine your own invention.

cool in hot weather

warm in cold weather

raincoat in wet weather

can change colour

looks like a TV   makes phone calls

plays music   sends emails

5 Happy holidays

deck

shopping mall

ice rink

whirlpool

climbing wall

gym

Reading

1 •05• **Read and listen.**

Oasis of the Seas is the biggest passenger ship in the world. The lucky passengers have got lots of activities to choose from. The ship has got sixteen decks. Each deck has got different areas or zones for passengers to visit.

The enormous shopping zone is called *The Royal Promenade*. There are lots of different shops and places to eat here. There is a shopping mall, lots of different restaurants and also some cafés. There are lots of different types of food to choose from – British, Italian, Chinese, Indian and others.

This is Central Park. It is the first ever living park at sea. It's amazing! This part of the ship hasn't got a roof. It's got lots of real trees and plants and it's a great place to relax.

There are lots of ways to keep fit on board. You can swim in four pools and ten whirlpools in the Pool Zone. In the Sports Zone, you can play basketball, climb rock walls or play mini-golf. Passengers can visit a gym and have some exercise classes, too. They can also have dance lessons or skate on an ice rink on the ship.

The Youth Zone is a great place for young children and teenagers. They can learn about science or art, or they can just relax and have lots of fun. *The Entertainment Place* is the zone where passengers can go in the evening. It's got two theatres and two cinemas. The bars and restaurants have got live music most nights.

Comprehension

2 Answer the questions.

1 How many decks are there on the ship? <u>There are sixteen decks.</u>

2 How many pools are there in the Pool Zone? _____

3 How many theatres are there on the ship? _____

4 How many whirlpools are there? _____

3 Copy the sentences into the table.

> ~~You can play basketball.~~
> Children can relax.
> There are lots of trees and plants.
> You can swim.
>
> There isn't a roof.
> You can find whirlpools.
> Children can learn about art.
> You can play mini-golf.

In the Youth Zone ...	In the Sports Zone ...
_____ _____ _____	<u>You can play</u> <u>basketball.</u> _____
In the Pool Zone ...	**In Central Park ...**
_____ _____ _____	_____ _____ _____

4 Read and write *Yes, there are.* or *No, there aren't.*

1 Are there any shops on the ship? <u>Yes, there are.</u>

2 Are there two ice rinks on the ship? _____

3 Are there any cafés in the Royal Promenade? _____

4 Are there any cars on the ship? _____

5 Are there any trees on the ship? _____

6 Are there twenty decks on the ship? _____

Vocabulary

5 Complete the sentences with the words in the box.

| climbing wall | deck | gym | ice rink | ~~shopping mall~~ | whirlpool |

1. You can buy clothes in the <u>shopping mall</u>.

2. I like sitting in the _____.

3. I love skating on the _____.

4. We're doing some exercise in the _____.

5. I enjoy using the _____.

6. It's sunny, so I'm relaxing on the _____.

6 Circle.

My family and I went to New York last month. We travelled on a huge plane. It was a very long [1] (journey) / passenger, but we took lots of books and [2] passports / magazines to read.
When we got to the [3] ship / airport in New York, we went to [4] arrivals / whirlpools and we waited for our [5] journey / luggage.
There were lots of other [6] suitcases / passengers waiting with us.
We found our bags and we went to our [7] deck / hotel.
It was a huge building, with a restaurant and a swimming [8] pool / wall. There was a gym in the hotel, so my mum had [9] science / exercise classes every day. My brother and I went to the [10] café / climbing wall with my dad and ate ice cream. It was a great holiday.

Writing

My dream hotel

My dream hotel is very big. It's got two pools and it's got a whirlpool, too. There's a gym and there's a basketball court. It hasn't got a tennis court because I don't like tennis.

You can eat lots of lovely food in my dream hotel because there is a great restaurant. There is a café in the hotel, too. You can buy delicious ice cream and cakes there. It's got play areas for children and quiet areas for adults. It's got a big cinema for everyone.

My dream hotel is a great place to relax. I hope I will go there one day!

7 Use the words to write sentences about a hotel.

1 My dream hotel / very big   <u>My dream hotel is very big.</u>

2 It's got / two restaurants / got / shop / too

_____

3 You can / lots of exercise / because / gym

_____

4 It's got / swimming pool / climbing wall

_____

5 There's / café / in / hotel / too

_____

6 You / buy / ice cream / cakes / there

_____

7 This hotel / great place / relax

_____

8 Write about your dream hotel in your notebook.

Use these words and phrases.

- *My dream hotel is …*
- *There's …*
- *You can …*
- *It's got …*
- *There are …*
- *It's a great place to …*
- *It hasn't got …*

6 Watching wildlife

| cameraman | lay eggs | balance | hatch | chick | feed |

Reading

1 📀 06 **Read and listen.**

March of the Penguins

In 2003, two French cameramen went to Antarctica to film emperor penguins for a year. Their fantastic film is called *March of the Penguins*.

Emperor penguins are amazing birds. They go on a very long and difficult journey every year. Hundreds of penguins get together and walk more than one hundred kilometres across the ice. They walk until they find a safe place for the mothers to lay eggs.

After they lay their eggs, the mothers give them to the fathers to look after. Then they walk back to the sea to find food for their new chicks. The fathers stay with the eggs. They balance the eggs carefully on their feet, because it is too cold on the ice. The fathers wait for sixty-four days for the eggs to hatch. They stand close together to keep warm in the snow and icy wind.

The mothers come back with food after two months. They feed the chicks while the fathers walk to the sea and back to find food for themselves. The parents make several journeys to find food until the chicks are about four months old. After that, the parents leave the chicks to look after themselves and return to the sea.

March of the Penguins is a very famous film. Lots of people all over the world went to watch it at the cinema. It's a documentary, but it's a wonderful story, too.

Comprehension

2 Complete the sentences with the words in the box.

| feed | film | find | leave | wait | walk |

1 The cameramen went to Antarctica to ___film___ penguins.

2 The penguins _____ more than 100 kilometres to find a safe place.

3 The fathers _____ sixty-four days for the eggs to hatch.

4 The mothers go to the sea to _____ food for the chicks.

5 The mothers return from the sea and _____ the chicks.

6 The parents _____ the chicks when they are about four months old.

3 Write a sentence from exercise 2 for each picture.

_____ _____ _____

_____ _____ _____

_____ _____ _____

4 Match the questions and the answers.

1 How many cameramen went to Antarctica?   Sixty-four days.

2 How far do the penguins walk?   Four months.

3 How long do the fathers wait for the eggs   One hundred
  to hatch?   kilometres.

4 How long do the mothers go away for?   Two.

5 How old are the chicks when their parents   Two months.
  return to the sea?

Vocabulary

5 Complete the definitions with the words in the box.

~~hatches~~ feed chick balance cameramen documentary journey lay

1 When an egg <u>hatches</u>, a chick comes out.

2 Female birds and fish _____ eggs when they push them from their bodies.

3 When you give food to someone, you _____ them.

4 When you _____ something, you put it somewhere carefully so it doesn't fall.

5 _____ use cameras to make films.

6 A _____ is a baby bird.

7 A _____ is a film about real life.

8 When you travel from one place to another, you make a _____.

6 Complete the text with the words in the box.

birds cartoon channel chicks documentary
hatch lay mother night ~~wildlife~~ fathers

I like watching TV shows about ¹ <u>wildlife</u> because I love animals. Last night, I watched a ² _____ about ostriches.

Ostriches are very big ³ _____. They live in hot countries. The father ostriches make a hole in the sand. The ⁴ _____ ostriches ⁵ _____ their eggs in the hole. Ostrich eggs are the biggest eggs in the world.

The mothers sit on the eggs in the day and the ⁶ _____ sit on the eggs at ⁷ _____. When the eggs ⁸ _____, the fathers look after the ⁹ _____.

It was a great programme, but I didn't see it all. My brother changed the ¹⁰ _____ because he wanted to watch a ¹¹ _____.

More words on page 46

Writing

Elephants

I once saw a documentary on TV about elephants. It was very interesting.
I learned that female elephants live in families, but male elephants leave the family. The males are unfriendly, they live on their own. When a family gets very big, some of the young females make a new group. They all care for the baby elephants.
Elephants are very unusual animals because they can use their noses to listen. They put their noses, or trunks, on the ground to hear sounds from a long way away. I saw this in the documentary too. They also use their trunks to make noises to communicate with other elephants.

7 Read the sentences and circle.

1 Chameleons are *usual* / *unusual* animals because they change colour.

2 Zoos are very *popular* / *unpopular* in Britain – lots of people visit them.

3 Something that doesn't make you laugh is *funny* / *unfunny*.

4 If you cry a lot you are *happy* / *unhappy*.

5 Sleeping on the floor is *comfortable* / *uncomfortable*.

6 Be careful with strange dogs as they can be *friendly* / *unfriendly*.

7 I am so *lucky* / *unlucky* – I am going on holiday tomorrow!

8 I love animal documentaries, they are *interesting* / *uninteresting*.

9 Caring for animals in danger is *important* / *unimportant*.

8 Write about a film or a book about animals in your notebook. Use these facts about gorillas or write about your favourite animal.

look unfriendly – are usually very gentle
live in family groups – strongest male looks after the group
clever – learn things easily
unusual – use sticks and rocks to do different jobs

Use these words and phrases.
• *I once saw / read …* • *I learned that …* • *… unusual animals because …*

7 Survival tips

hill

branch

boil

insects

insect repellent

happy thoughts

Reading

1 07 Read and listen.

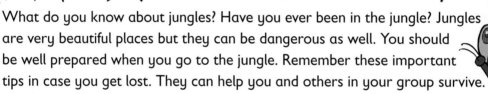

What do you know about jungles? Have you ever been in the jungle? Jungles are very beautiful places but they can be dangerous as well. You should be well prepared when you go to the jungle. Remember these important tips in case you get lost. They can help you and others in your group survive.

1 Find a hill Climb a hill so that you can see over the top of the trees. When you've found a hill, look to see if there is a river. You can follow the river out of the jungle to safety.

2 Make a safe camp Find a dry place, but don't camp very near trees. It isn't safe to camp near trees because trees and branches can sometimes fall.

3 Keep insects away Wear strong insect repellent to keep dangerous insects away. Always look in your shoes before you put them on. Some insects like to hide in shoes and they will bite or sting you.

4 Drink lots of clean water It's hot in the jungle, so it's important to drink enough water. Have you run out of water? Boil some water from a river to make it clean and safe to drink.

5 Try to think happy thoughts It's very important to stay cheerful. Think about how you will feel when you are safe with your family again. Try not to worry too much.

6 Look up at the sky The sun and the stars can help you to find your way out of the jungle.

Remember these tips and your trip to the jungle will be a lot safer!

Comprehension

2 Read and tick (✔) or cross (✗).

1 It's a good idea to look for a river.   ✔

2 You need to make a camp in a wet place.   ☐

3 It's important to check your shoes before you put them on.   ☐

4 It's important to drink clean water.   ☐

5 You mustn't boil water from rivers.   ☐

3 Match. Write the number.

1 Find a hill.

2 Make a safe camp.

3 Drink lots of water.

4 Think happy thoughts.

5 Always look in your shoes.

6 Don't camp near trees.

a

b

c

d

e

f   1

4 Circle the correct answers.

1 Can you follow a river out of the jungle?   (Yes, you can.) / No, you can't.

2 Is it safe to camp near trees?   Yes, it is. / No, it isn't.

3 Do trees sometimes fall in the jungle?   Yes, they do. / No, they don't.

4 Can the sun help you find your way in the jungle?   Yes, it can. / No, it can't.

5 Is it important to stay cheerful?   Yes, it is. / No, it isn't.

Vocabulary

5 Match the definitions with the words in the box.

| insects branch boil insect repellent hill jungle |
| cheerful ~~run out~~ volcano camp |

1 When there is nothing left of something. <u>run out</u>

2 Part of a tree. _____

3 To heat water until it becomes steam. _____

4 Small animals such as flies, ants and mosquitoes. _____

5 Something you use to keep insects away. _____

6 How to describe someone who smiles and is happy. _____

7 Another word for rainforest. _____

8 An area of land higher than land around it. _____

9 A type of mountain that can erupt fire and lava. _____

10 The place where someone puts a tent or shelter. _____

6 Complete the sentences. Match.

| desert   island   ~~jungle~~   mountains   river   volcano |

1 The girl in the red jumper is in the <u>jungle</u>.

2 The boys in green T-shirts are walking next to the _____.

3 The boy in the orange jumper is looking at the _____.

4 The girls in white dresses are looking at the _____.

5 The boys in black jumpers are having a picnic on an _____.

6 The boy in the blue T-shirt is in the _____.

More words on page 47

Writing

Tips for survival in the mountains

Have you ever been to the mountains? It's very exciting, but there are some important things to remember.

1 Have you told someone about your trip?
It's a good idea to leave a map of your trip with a friend or relative.

2 Have you packed the right things?
Think carefully about what to take. You will need a torch, a map, some water, some food and insect repellent.

3 Have you chosen the right clothes?
It's very cold in the mountains, so you will need warm clothes. Make sure you have some comfortable shoes and some thick socks.

4 Have you read some mountain survival tips?
Read a book about mountain survival tips. Then you will know what to do in an emergency.

7 Complete the advice with the words in the box.

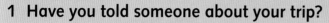

about   ~~good~~   need   sure   very

Survival in the desert	
It's a _good_ idea	to travel with a friend.
It's _____ important	to drink lots of water.
You will _____	light clothes and a sun hat.
Make _____ you have	suncream.
Read a book _____	survival in the desert.

8 Write tips for survival in the desert in your notebook.

Write questions with *Have you…?*:
Have you read some desert survival tips?

Write answers to your questions. Use these words and phrases.
• *It's a good idea to…* • *It's important to…* • *Make sure you have…* • *You will need…*

8 Growing things

soil   seeds   bulbs   rake   dig   pots

Reading

1 08 Read and listen.

A vegetable garden

Have you got a garden? Do you help your parents or grandparents in the garden? So why not grow your own vegetables? We should all eat lots of vegetables to be healthy and growing vegetables is a lot of fun.

You should always plant vegetables in a sunny place and in good soil. You shouldn't plant vegetables outside when the weather is cold, because they won't grow.

What is your favourite vegetable? What vegetables does your family like to eat? Choose the vegetables you want to grow. Tomatoes, onions, corn and beans are easy to grow and they all taste really great. For tomatoes, you can plant seeds or small plants. For onions, you can plant bulbs. Plant lots of different ones – then you can see which you and your family like best! Some of them will grow better than others in your garden. You should draw a picture of your vegetable garden so you can remember where you planted your different vegetables. Then you will know what they are when they start to grow.

You should rake and water the soil and dig some small holes. Then plant your seeds or vegetable plants in the holes. You should water your vegetable plants every day. The best time to water them is in the morning. Ask a friend or someone in your family to water them when you can't do it.

You don't need a big garden to grow vegetables. You could also grow them in big pots. And when your vegetables are ready, you can pick them, wash them, cook them and eat them! So, why not start your vegetable garden today?

Comprehension

2 Read and tick (✔) or cross (✘).

1 Tomatoes are difficult to grow. ☒

2 You should plant your vegetables when the weather is cold. ☐

3 A picture will help you to remember where you planted your different vegetables. ☐

4 It's best to water vegetable plants in the morning. ☐

5 You must have a big garden to grow vegetables. ☐

6 You could grow vegetables in pots. ☐

3 Write a sentence from the text for each picture.

We should all eat lots of vegetables to be healthy.

_____

_____

_____

_____

_____

_____

4 Match the questions and the answers.

1 Why should we eat lots of vegetables?

2 Which vegetables are easy to grow?

3 Where should I plant vegetables?

4 Why shouldn't I plant vegetables outside in cold weather?

5 When should I water my vegetable garden?

The best time is in the morning.

Tomatoes, onions, corn and beans.

Because it's healthy.

In a sunny place.

Because they won't grow.

Vocabulary

5 Read the definitions and circle.

1 A container you can grow plants in is a (pot)/ pan.

2 Part of a plant that is underground from which vegetables like onions grow is a *leaf* / *bulb*.

3 The small, hard parts of a plant you put in the ground to grow more plants are called *seeds* / *soil*.

4 You *dig* / *rake* holes in the soil with a spade.

5 If you eat lots of vegetables you will be *hungry* / *healthy*.

6 When your vegetables are grown and ready to eat, you *rake* / *pick* them.

6 Complete the text with the words in the box.

beans	cabbage	corn	dig	holes	plant	rake	seeds	soil	~~water~~

We're all working in the garden this morning. Karen is going to ¹ <u>water</u> the flowers. Tom is going to ² _____ some new tomato plants.

Lisa is going to ³ _____ part of the garden to make the ⁴ _____ soft. Then Sam is going to ⁵ _____ lots of small ⁶ _____ in the soil. They're going to put some ⁷ _____ in the holes and grow some plants.

Emma has just picked some ⁸ _____. Now she's going to pick some ⁹ _____.

I'm picking a big ¹⁰ _____. We're going to have lots of vegetables for lunch.

More words on page 47

Writing

How to grow a bulb in a bottle

The best time to grow bulbs is in the spring. We usually plant bulbs in the garden or in a pot, but you can plant a bulb in a bottle.

First, you have to fill a bottle with water and put the bulb on top of the bottle.

Next, you should cover the bottle with a paper bag. You have to put it in a dark cupboard so the bulb can start to grow. Then, you should move it to a sunny place, because flowers need sunshine. You should put more water in the bottle every few days. You have to do this carefully, because you shouldn't move the bulb much.

A bulb in a bottle is a great way to grow pretty flowers.

7 Match the sentence halves about growing sunflowers.

1 You should plant seeds in warm weather   so they don't fall over.

2 You shouldn't plant seeds close together   because sunflowers need lots of sun.

3 You should water the seeds every day   the sunflowers won't grow.

4 You shouldn't let the soil get dry because   so they grow into strong plants.

5 You should put tall sticks behind the plants   because sunflowers need room to grow.

6 You should grow some sunflowers   so your garden looks pretty.

8 Write about how to grow sunflowers in your notebook. Use the information in exercise 7 to help.

Use these words and phrases.
• The best time to …   • First, …   • Next, …   • Then, …
• You should …   • You shouldn't … because   • It's a good idea to … so

9 Heroes

dive   drag   trapped   escape   rescue   put out

Reading

1 🔊09 Read and listen.

These newspaper articles tell the stories of three very brave young people from different parts of the world and why they are heroes.

A hero and a friend

Haden Stusak is from Atlanta in the USA. One day, he was playing in his grandma's swimming pool with his best friend, Josiah. Haden was practising diving when he saw Josiah at the bottom of the pool. He was drowning. The adults did not see him. "I was the only person who saw him," said Haden. Haden, who is six years old, quickly dived into the pool. He dragged five-year-old Josiah out of the water. A few minutes later Josiah was breathing again.

Everyone called Haden a hero. "I'm not a hero," said Haden. "I'm just a good friend."

Earthquake hero

Nine-year-old Lin Hao from China was having a Maths lesson with thirty of his classmates when there was a huge earthquake. The school building started to fall down. Lin and his classmates were trapped inside.

Lin was able to escape, but his friends were still in the building. Lin went back into the building three times to rescue them. "It was my job to look after my classmates", he said.

Good neighbours

Kiah Kurtzer, who is from Australia, was looking out of her bedroom window one night when she saw that her neighbour's bin was on fire. Fourteen-year-old Kiah first called the fire brigade, then she ran outside to start to put the fire out. She used water from the garden hose to put out the fire. Her neighbour came to help her. When the fire brigade arrived, the fire was already out.

"I was scared," said Kiah, "but I think it's important to help your neighbours."

Comprehension

2 Tick (✔) the correct sentences.

1 a Haden saw his friend at the bottom of the pool. ✔

  b Haden's friend saw him at the bottom of the pool. ☐

2 a Josiah dragged Haden out of the pool. ☐

  b Haden dragged Josiah out of the pool. ☐

3 a Kiah was at her neighbour's house when she saw the fire. ☐

  b Kiah was at home when she saw the fire. ☐

4 a Kiah used water to put out the fire. ☐

  b The fire brigade put out the fire. ☐

5 a The earthquake started when Lin was in a Maths lesson. ☐

  b Lin wasn't at school when the earthquake started. ☐

6 a Lin escaped from the building. ☐

  b Lin's classmates rescued him from the building. ☐

7 a Lin didn't go back into the building. ☐

  b Lin went back into the building. ☐

3 Match the sentences to the people who said them.

1 "We were still in the building. Lin Hao came back and rescued us,"

2 "The boys were playing in my swimming pool. I wasn't watching them,"

3 "I need a new bin now, but I'm very happy. Thank you, Kiah,"

4 "He dived into the pool and saved me. He's a hero,"

5 "All the children were brave, but Lin Hao was the bravest,"

6 "I didn't think about the earthquake. I wanted to rescue my friends,"

said Lin Hao.

said Haden's grandmother.

said Lin Hao's friends.

said Lin Hao's teacher.

said Josiah.

said Kiah's neighbour.

Vocabulary

4 Circle.

1 The fire brigade arrived and (put out)/ *fell down* the fire.

2 How did you *help / escape* from the building?

3 Come on! Let's *drag / dive* into the swimming pool.

4 Brave firefighters *escaped / rescued* everyone in the building.

5 This box is heavy. Can you help me *drag / find* it to the door?

6 I can't move! I'm *trapped / dragged*.

5 Complete the texts with the words in the boxes.

| pulled | arrived | dived | ~~called~~ | fell |

Tom was walking by the river when he saw two little boys. The boys [1] _called_ to Tom. "Help! Our toy car [2] _____ into the river and we can't get it."

Tom quickly [3] _____ into the river and he [4] _____ the car out of the water. The boys were very happy. Just then, the boys' father [5] _____. He said "Thank you very much." to Tom.

| climb | rescue | trapped | noise | escape |

Kelly was in her bedroom when she heard a [6] _____. She looked out of her bedroom window and saw that her neighbours' cat was in a tree in her garden. The cat was [7] _____ in the tree. It couldn't [8] _____ because the branch was very high.

Kelly went outside. She used a ladder to [9] _____ up and get the cat. Soon, the cat was safe and Kelly's neighbours were very happy.

"It's a very pretty cat," said Kelly. "I'm glad I could [10] _____ it."

More words on page 48

Writing

My hero

My hero is Jake Sanders. Jake, who lives next door to us, is a taxi driver. We've known him since my family moved to this street five years ago.

I think Jake is a hero because he helped me and my mum when we lost our keys. We arrived home from the supermarket and we couldn't open the front door. Jake saw us and went to find a ladder. He climbed up to the bathroom window, which was open. Then he climbed through the window and opened the door for us.

Jake is very kind and he is nice to everyone. I think Jake is an amazing person. I'm very glad that he's our neighbour.

6 Rewrite the sentences with commas.

1 Mike who lives next door is my best friend.

   Mike, who lives next door, is my best friend.

2 Their house which is near the park is very big.

   _____

3 The children who were walking to school called for help.

   _____

4 Ben's dad who is a firefighter saved the family.

   _____

5 This building which is very old is going to fall down.

   _____

7 Write about your hero in your notebook.

Use these words and phrases.
- *My hero is …*
- *I've known him / her since …*
- *I think he / she is a hero because …*
- *He / She is very …*

10 Story time

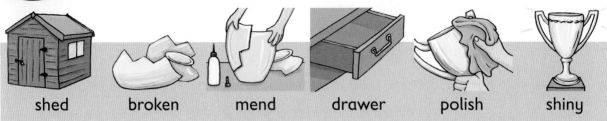

| shed | broken | mend | drawer | polish | shiny |

Reading

1 🔊10 **Read and listen.**

Grandpa's new bike

Anna and Jack were staying at their grandpa's house for the weekend. They were looking at some old photos when they found a photo of a teenage boy with a fantastic new bike. "Who's that boy, Grandpa?" asked Anna. Grandpa looked at the photo and laughed.

"That's me over fifty years ago," he said. "I really loved that bike. It's in my shed, but it's old and broken now."

Grandpa went shopping. While he was out Jack had an idea. "Grandpa hasn't got a bike. Let's mend his old bike for him!" he said.

Jack and Anna ran to Grandpa's shed and looked around.

"Look!" said Anna and pointed to an old bike.

"It's a great bike," Jack said. "But look – one of the wheels has fallen off."

Anna found some tools in a drawer and they mended the wheel. They cleaned and polished the bike so it looked new again. They worked very quickly because they did not have much time.

Then they heard a voice outside. Grandpa was back from the shops.

"Anna! Jack! Where are you?"

"It's Grandpa!" said Anna.

Anna and Jack went outside and showed Grandpa the bike. He was amazed and very happy.

"That's my old bike," he said. "But it looks new and shiny."

"Yes. We mended it," said Jack. "We put the wheel back on, and polished it for you."

Grandpa was very pleased and excited.

"Let's ride our bikes together this afternoon," he said.

Anna and Jack were very happy. They all rode their bikes to the park and had a wonderful picnic in the sunshine.

Comprehension

2 Complete the sentences with the words in the box.

found	mended	had	rode	~~showed~~	heard

1 Anna and Jack __showed__ Grandpa a photo.

2 Jack _____ an idea.

3 Anna _____ some tools in a drawer.

4 Anna and Jack _____ the bike.

5 Anna and Jack _____ a voice outside the shed.

6 They all _____ their bikes to the park.

3 Match the sentence halves.

1 Anna and Jack were staying at Grandpa's house   while Grandpa was out.

2 Jack had an idea   Anna and Jack were in the shed.

3 When they looked in the shed   he was amazed.

4 When Grandpa came back from shopping,   because Anna and Jack cleaned it.

5 When Grandpa saw his old bike   when they found a photo.

6 The bike looked shiny and new   they found Grandpa's old bike.

7 They were all very happy when   they rode their bikes to the park.

4 Correct the words in bold.

1 Anna and Jack were looking at some old **letters**.   _photos_

2 Grandpa **cried** when he saw the photo.   _____

3 Grandpa's bike was **new** and broken.   _____

4 Anna and Jack heard a **noise** outside.   _____

5 When Grandpa saw the bike, he was **worried**.   _____

6 They all had a picnic in the **rain**.   _____

Vocabulary

5 Complete the sentences.

One day, when Mum was tidying the ¹ <u>shed</u>, she found an old toy. It

was a doll's ² _____ she played with when she was a little girl. It

was dirty and it had ³ _____ doors and windows, but she decided

to ⁴ _____ it for me. She fixed the doors and windows and

⁵ _____ it until it looked all ⁶ _____ and new. She found

a doll in a ⁷ _____ in my bedroom and put her into the house. I was

so surprised when I got home from school!

6 Complete the definitions with the words in the box.

amazed	broken	cupboard	drawer	mend
shed	shiny	tools	voice	wheels

1   <u>Amazed</u> means very surprised.

2   We can use _____ to make or mend things.

3   When you polish a car, it looks new and _____.

4   When something is _____, it doesn't work.

5   A bike has two _____.

6   When you make a broken thing work again, you _____ it.

7   A _____ is a small building in a garden.

8   You use your _____ to speak or sing.

9   We keep our knives, forks and spoons in a _____.

10 We keep our plates and cups in a _____.

More words on page 48

Writing

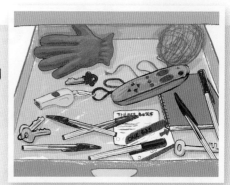

My safe place

One Saturday morning, Mum said to Ben, "Please tidy your bedroom."

Ben went upstairs but a few minutes later he came downstairs again. Mum was reading.

"My bedroom is tidy now," he said.

"Good," said Mum. "Take some money from the drawer and buy an ice cream."

Ben opened the drawer. He took out six pens, some string, four keys, one glove, a whistle, two bus tickets, a notebook and an old remote control.

"What are all these things?" asked Ben

"Oh, that's my safe place," said Mum. "Let's go and see your room."

They went upstairs to Ben's bedroom. It looked nice and tidy. Then Mum looked under Ben's bed. All Ben's clothes, books and toys were under his bed.

"What are all these things?" she asked.

"That's my safe place," said Ben.

Mum laughed. "Let's tidy your room," she said. "Then we can tidy my drawer."

7 Rewrite the sentences with punctuation.

1   I want you to tidy your bedroom Mum said <u>"I want you to tidy your bedroom," Mum said.</u>

2   Theres someone in the garden he said _____

3   This is our new house they said _____

4   Where are you going she asked _____

8 Write a story in your notebook.

Use a time expression to begin your story:
One day, … One afternoon, … One Saturday morning, …
Use the past simple and the past continuous:
Later, he came downstairs. His mum was reading.
Use speech marks, commas and question marks when someone is speaking:
"My bedroom is tidy now," he said. "What are all these things?" asked Ben.

More words

1 Eating round the world

oven   oven gloves   oven dish   saucepan   frying pan

Complete the sentences.

1   You can cook meat and vegetables in an _____.

2   You can cook vegetables in hot water in a _____.

3   To make bread, you need a hot _____.

4   You can fry meat in a _____.

5   Oven dishes are often very hot. You must wear _____.

2 Making music

microphone   speakers   electric guitar   keyboard   drum sticks

Complete the puzzle and find the mystery word.

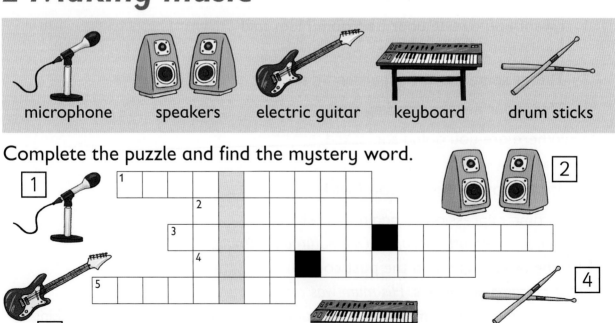

3 My favourite sport

 football boots    hockey stick    tennis racket    swimming costume    ski goggles

Complete the sentences.

1. I've got my _____.
   I'm going to play hockey.

2. I've got my _____.
   I'm going to play football.

3. I've got my _____.
   I'm going to play tennis.

4. I've got my _____.
   I'm going to go swimming.

5. I've got my _____. I'm going to go skiing.

4 Future inventions

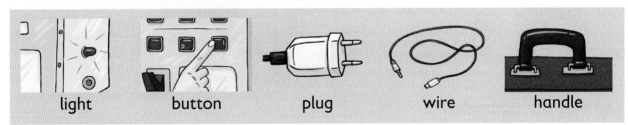

light   button   plug   wire   handle

Complete the text.

Look at this amazing machine.

It's got a big [1] _____, so you can carry it.

It's white and it's got lots of red [2] _____.

There are three [3] _____ on the side of the machine.

They are red, orange and green.

The machine's got a long black [4] _____.

At the end of the wire, there's a white [5] _____.

5 Happy holidays

| porthole | anchor | flag | harbour | lighthouse |

Match. Find the words and circle.

a

b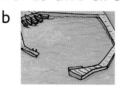

c

d

e

f

1 e d h a r b o u r k

2 t a n c h o r p f

3 p o r t h o l e q v p d

4 d f m d e c k v

5 p l i g h t h o u s e l

6 r t y f l a g f

6 Watching wildlife

| gorilla | dolphin | wolf | bear | polar bear |

Answer the questions.

1   It's big. It's brown or black. It can be dangerous.

2   It's big. It lives in a very cold place. It's white.

3   This big animal lives in the forest, in hot countries.
    It eats fruit.

4   It looks like a dog but it's more dangerous.
    It eats meat. What is it?

5   This clever animal is not dangerous.
    It is an amazing swimmer.

7 Survival tips

camel   sand dunes   water bottle   oasis   scorpion

Write and match.

1   The wind in the desert makes
    _____.

2   When we went to the desert, I
    rode a _____.

3   I once picked up a rock and found
    a _____.

4   When you travel in the desert,
    always carry a _____.

5   There are trees and a lake at
    an _____.

a

b

c

d

e

8 Growing things

greenhouse   watering can   seedlings   trowel   fork

Complete the puzzle and find the mystery word.

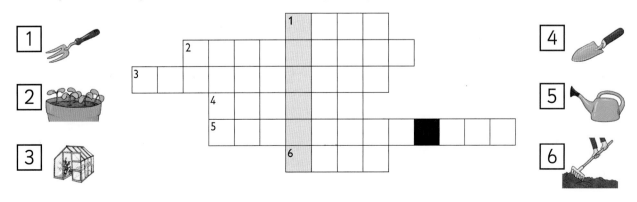

9 Heroes

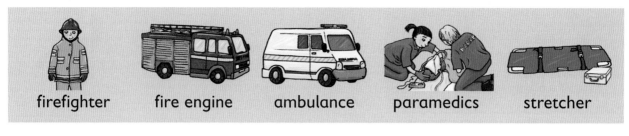

firefighter   fire engine   ambulance   paramedics   stretcher

Complete the puzzle.

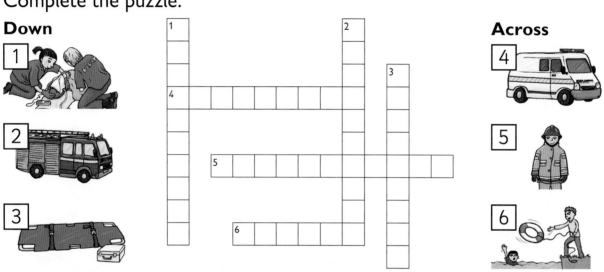

Down

1
2
3

Across

4
5
6

10 Story time

think   whisper   ask   laugh   shout

Complete the sentences with the words in the box.

asked
laughed
shouted
thought
whispered

1 'It's dark. I'm scared,' _____ Joe.

2 'That's a funny hat!' _____ Nick.

3 'I'm going to mend Mum's old bike,'
_____ Sally.

4 'Have you got a watering can?' _____
Emma.

5 'Run! There's a gorilla!' _____ Bob.